A World of Difference

Toys Everywhere

By Cynthia Hedges Greising and David Greising

CHILDRENS PRESS®
CHICAGO

Picture Acknowledgements

Cover (top left), NASA; cover (bottom left), © Tom McCarthy Photos/Unicorn Stock Photos; cover (top right), © Robert Frerck/Odyssey/Chicago; cover (bottom right), © Reinhard Brucker; 1, © John Elk III; 3 (left), © Robert Frerck/Odyssey/Chicago; 3 (top right), © Reinhard Brucker/Field Museum, Chicago; 3 (bottom right), © Wolfgang Kaehler; 4 (left), © Cameramann International, Ltd.; 4 (right), © Robert Frerck/Odyssey/Chicago; 5 (left), © Tony Freeman/PhotoEdit; 5 (top right), © Wendy Stone/Odyssey/Chicago; 5 (bottom right), © Lani Novak Howe/Photri; 6 (left), © Robert Frerck/Odyssey/Chicago; 6 (top right), © J. Bisley/Unicorn Stock Photos; 6 (bottom right); The Metropolitan Museum of Art, Rogers Fund, 1940.(40.2.1); 7 (left), © Carl Purcell; 7 (right), The Bettmann Archive; 8 (top), © Wanda Christl/Root Resources; 8 (bottom), H. Armstrong Roberts; 9 (top left), © Thomas Wagner/Odyssey/Chicago; 9 (bottom left), © Reinhard Brucker; 9 (center), H. Armstrong Roberts; 9 (right), © Robert Frerck/Odyssey/Chicago; 10 (left), H. Armstrong Roberts; 10 (right), SuperStock International, Inc.; 11 (top left), © Wolfgang Kaehler; 11 (bottom left), © Robert Frerck/Odyssey/Chicago; 11 (right), © S. Winter/Unicorn Stock Photos; 12 (bottom left), © Victor Englebert; 12 (top right), © Reinhard Brucker/Milwaukee Public Museum; 12 (bottom right), Reinhard Brucker; 13 (top left), © Virginia R. Grimes; 13 (bottom), © Robert Frerck/Odyssey/Chicago; 13 (top right), © Wolfgang Kaehler; 14 (bottom left), © Victor Englebert; 14 (bottom right), © Robert Frerck/Odyssey/Chicago; 14 (top right), © Victor Englebert; 15 (top and bottom), © Wolfgang Kaehler; 16 (bottom left), © Bill Aron/PhotoEdit; 16 (bottom right), © Robert Frerck/Odyssey/Chicago; 16 (top right), © David Hiser/Tony Stone Images; 17 (top), © Robert Frerck/Odyssey/Chicago; 17 (bottom), © John Callahan/Tony Stone Images; 18 (left), © Robert Frerck/Odyssey/Chicago; 18 (top right), © Wendy Stone/Odyssey/Chicago; 18 (bottom right), © Reinhard Brucker/Field Museum, Chicago; 19 (bottom right), © David Hiser/Tony Stone Images; 20 (left), © Mary A. Root/Root Resources; 20 (right), © Victor Englebert; 21 (top left), © John Elk III; 21 (bottom left and right), © Wolfgang Kaehler; 22 (left), © Tom McCarthy/MGA/Photri; 22 (right), © Kennon Cooke/Valan; 23 (top), Photri; 23 (bottom left and right), © Reinhard Brucker; 24 (left), © John Eastcott/Yva Momatiuk/Valan; 24 (right), © Robert Frerck/Odyssey/Chicago; 25 (top), SuperStock International, Inc.; 25 (center), AP/Wide World Photos; 25 (bottom), © Reinhard Brucker; 26 (left), © Robert Frerck/Odyssey/Chicago; 26 (right), © Virginia R. Grimes; 27 (left), © Victor Englebert; 27 (right), © Robert Frerck/Odyssey/Chicago; 28 (left), © Victor Englebert; 28 (right), © Robert Frerck/Odyssey/Chicago; 29 (left), Chip and Rosa Maria de la Cueva Peterson; 29 (top right), © Wolfgang Kaehler; 29 (bottom right), © Ann Purcell; 30 (left), © Gay Bumgarner/Tony Stone Images; 30 (right), © Jeff Greenberg/Unicorn Stock Photos; 31 (top), © Wolfgang Kaehler; 31 (center), Reuters/Bettmann; 31 (bottom), © Laura Dwight

On the cover

Top: Clay truck, Colombia
Bottom left: Boy with plastic ball, United States
Bottom right: Iroquois corn-husk doll

On the title page

Wooden helicopter, Botswana

Project Editor Shari Joffe
Design Herman Adler Design Group
Photo Research Feldman & Associates, Inc.

Library of Congress Cataloging-in-Publication Data

Greising, Cynthia Hedges.
    Toys everywhere / by Cynthia Hedges Greising & David Greising.
        p. cm. — (A world of difference)
    Includes bibliographical references.
    Summary: Describes a variety of toys from around the world, including the Australian boomerang, South African knobkerrie, and Japanese daruma doll.
    ISBN 0-516-08178-0 (lib. bdg.)—ISBN 0-516-48178-9 (pbk.)
    1. Toys — Juvenile literature. [1. Toys.] I. Greising, David, 1960 – .
II. Title. III. Series.
GV 1218.5.G72 1995
790.1'33 — dc20

95-16256
CIP
AC MN

Contents

Everyone Loves Toys

If you could choose how to spend an entire day, what would you do? Go to school? Clean your bedroom? Or play with your friends? If you chose playing, you picked something that young people all over the world like to do.

People play all their lives. And the objects they play with are toys. When you were a newborn baby, a brightly colored mobile over your crib or a rattle were probably your first toys. As a toddler, you may have played with blocks and puzzles. Now you may like riding a skateboard, throwing a ball, or flying a kite.

Clay toy truck, Colombia

It may seem like toys are just for fun, but they are really much more important than that. Toys help kids learn about the world around them, they help teach kids how to get along with others, and they help strengthen kids' minds and bodies! That is why toys are a part of every culture around the world.

Many kinds of toys—like balls, blocks, puzzles, and dolls—are found all over the world. But lots of cultures also have their own kinds of toys! In some countries, kids play with toys like animal bones or clay dolls. Children in Burma shoot pieces of dry mud in slingshots. Japanese kids play with complex computer games.

Diablo, Taiwan The *diablo* is a spinning toy that originated in China. This Taiwanese boy pulls up and down on the sticks to make the *diablo* spin up and down on the string. He tosses and catches the *diablo* in the air while it is still spinning.

Hula hoop, Kenya Hoops have been popular toys since the time of ancient Greece. But nobody in Greece ever thought to invent the hula hoop. The hula hoop helps teach physical coordination. It was a craze in the 1950s, when children all over the United States tried to keep it spinning around their waists for as long as they could. Now hula hoops can be found all over the world.

Piñata, **Mexico** You couldn't invent a better combination—a toy and candy all in one! *Piñatas* are popular at children's birthday parties and other celebrations. Kids put on a blindfold and try to whack the *piñata* with a stick while an adult nearby moves it up and down with a rope. One good hit, and the candy inside spills out!

Stuffed lions, Germany "Pretending" toys—like stuffed animals, dolls, and puppets—encourage children to talk, and teach them to use their imaginations.

Do you remember having a favorite toy as a small child? Was it a stuffed animal, a toy train, or a truck? You may discover it is quite similar to a toy loved by someone in another part of the world!

Toys for All Times

As long as there have been kids, there have been toys. Even in prehistoric times, people probably made toy dolls from wood or bone, and dressed them in scraps of fur.

The oldest toys ever found were made 3,000 years ago—and you thought some of your toys were getting old! When archaeologists were digging up a temple in Iran, they found a toy porcupine and toy lion carved out of limestone. The animals were on wheels, so some kid many centuries ago must have pulled them around just like children do today.

Through the centuries, toys have been almost a mirror of what's going on in the world. In the Middle Ages, when knights in shining armor roamed Europe, kids in England and Germany played with toy knights. Japanese children played with little *samurai* warriors.

Toy medieval knight
During the Middle Ages, mounted warriors called knights fought battles dressed in metal suits called armor. Kids played with miniature knights just like they play with toy soldiers today. They even had pretend jousts, trying to knock their friends' knights off their horses.

Prehistoric clay whistle, Mexico
Whistles are thought to be among the oldest clay toys. They have been found at ancient Indian burial sites in Mexico.

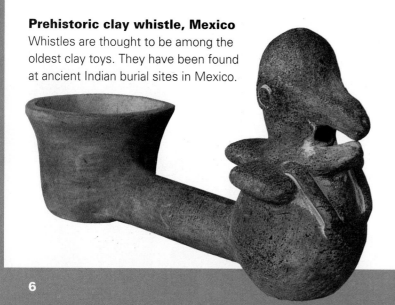

Kite, China The kite was invented 2,000 years ago in China. Back then, kites were not only toys, but also were used to send messages during wartime. In Japan, poor people used to like flying kites over the castles of rich people. If they couldn't know what it was like to be rich, at least their kites could get a peek!

French doll, 1700s
Toys are often influenced by what's going on in a country politically. During the French Revolution, French children played with dolls dressed in revolutionary fashion.

For a while, toys called automata were a big deal in Europe. They were wind-up toys, with figures like ballerinas or monkeys banging drums. During the 1700s, the French made some automata that were so huge, adults could fit on them. French ruler Napoleon played chess with an automaton one time, but he was faked out! It turned out a real person had dressed up as a toy.

Ancient Egyptian ivory dog, c. 400 B.C.
Kids have always liked toys with moving parts. This wooden dog has a hinged mouth that moves up and down when a lever is pulled.

The minute some new invention came along, kids would get a new kind of toy. In the 1800s, steam engines were invented, and guess what? Kids started playing with steam-driven toy trains. In the 1950s, the Russians sent the *Sputnik* rockets into space, and *Sputnik* toys suddenly became popular.

Toys got a lot more complex over the years. That's because toymakers switched from carving and metal-working to mass production. Throughout most of history, toys were made by parents or craftsworkers. In Germany in the mid-1800s, toys started being produced in large factories. For a long time, most manufactured toys were made of tin—everything from miniature cars to robots. Around the time your parents were growing up, plastic toys became popular. Today, most toys are made of plastic. And a lot of today's toys use tiny electronics that weren't even around twenty years ago.

Miniature steam-engine trains Toy trains have been popular since the first trains were invented in the early 1800s. Some of the neatest were actual steam-powered trains that came along during the late 1800s, when many people in Germany and other countries began traveling by train.

1920s toy car, United States Throughout history, people have made toys that reflect the newest technology of the time. This toy car is from the 1920s, when, for the first time, automobiles became affordable and Americans began buying them in large numbers.

Into the Space Age When space travel first began, in the 1950s, people became fascinated with space-age toys. Some of the most popular were robots, like this Japanese model (above); and military or space rockets, like this American rocket (right).

Subcommander Marcos doll, Mexico Here's a recent example of how toys can be influenced by politics. This handmade doll represents the man known as Subcommander Marcos, a hero to the Mayan Indians of Chiapas, Mexico. In 1994, he led a revolt against the region's landowners, who had long been unfair to the Mayan people who worked for them. Like Marcos, the doll wears a black bandanna to conceal his identity.

Troll, Denmark Toy makers have used different materials at different times in history. In European countries over the years, toy materials changed from clay and rocks to wood to metal to plastic. The people of Denmark have always had superstitions about creatures that live in the woods. Some believe that plastic troll dolls like these will bring them luck!

First a Tool, Then a Toy

Imagine using a toy to fight an enemy or to get your dinner. Strange as it may seem, some popular toys were first used as weapons or hunting tools. People in the Philippines once used the yo-yo to attack their enemies on the head! These days, if a yo-yo bonks somebody on the head, it's probably because someone was trying a crazy trick.

In cultures that rely on catching animals for food, toy hunting tools help children learn skills they will need as adults.

The Xhosa people live in South Africa. Xhosa boys use sticks called *knobkerrie* for hunting birds and other animals. But at playtime, they gather together in large circles and battle against friends with their sticks.

The boomerang, invented by the Aboriginal people of Australia, was originally used as a hunting weapon. But the Aborigines also use the boomerang as a tool for cutting and scraping—and as a toy. They even strike two boomerangs together to make music. Whew! Boomerangs are some of the hardest-working toys in the world.

Yo-yo *Yo-yo* is a Filipino word that means "come back." Yo-yos are now one of the most popular toys in the world. But not all people call this toy a yo-yo. In France, it's a *bandelure,* or "winding toy." And in some other parts of Europe it is called a *quiz.*

Native American slingshot A slingshot is a forked stick with an elastic band attached for hurling small rocks or pellets. Though many people think of it as a toy, it is also one of the oldest known weapons, and can be found in cultures all over the world.

Toy bow and arrow, Cambodia In cultures that rely on catching animals for food, toy hunting tools can help children learn skills they will need as adults.

Boomerang, Australia Talk about a great idea! Boomerangs are toys that come back no matter how hard you throw them. That's because the two legs of the boomerang work like wings that make the toy fly in a circle. Hunters in Australia discovered that the spinning legs of the boomerang conked birds on the head a lot harder than stones could. Today, people in Australia love competing in boomerang-throwing contests.

Toy windmills, Portugal Most people think of Holland when they think of windmills, but windmills are used to pump water in the hilly country of Portugal, too. Portuguese children like to place toy windmills near open windows. They catch the wind and spin, just like the real thing.

Clay, Wood, or Plastic?

Just what are toys made of, anyway? Depends on where you live, and where you get your toys. In fact, what your toys are made of can tell you a lot about the place where you live.

People choose different materials for different reasons. Sometimes, they just pick up the easiest thing around. In a place like Germany, there are many forests. So Germans make lots of wooden toys. There aren't many trees in the arctic circle, so Inuit people make toys out of walrus tusks.

Millet-stem car, Benin Millet, a grain that can be grown in hot, dry climates, is a common crop in the African country of Benin. So it's not surprising that kids there often make toys out of millet stems!

Inuit ivory seal The Inuit people live in the arctic regions of North America and in Greenland. If there weren't walruses around, Inuit kids would miss out on a lot of toys. That's because they make lots of their toys out of walrus tusks.

Iroquois corn-husk doll Traditionally, corn was an important crop for the Iroquois people of eastern North America.

Animal-bone game, Mongolia In Mongolia, which is largely rural, many people make their living raising sheep, camels, and cattle. Mongolian children play several kinds of games that use animal bones for game pieces.

Wooden oxcart, Germany Wood remains a durable and valued material for making toys. Many wooden toys are still made in Germany, a land of many forests.

Boy playing with turtle shell, Caroline Islands Wherever they may live, kids are great at making toys out of whatever they find around them!

Many times, new inventions make new kinds of toys possible. In the 1930s, as machines got better at stamping out metal, metal cars and trucks became popular in the United States. It was a lot easier than carving them from wood.

Today, in countries where kids get most of their toys from stores, many toys are made from plastic. Check out your own toys and see. It's easy and cheap to make large numbers of plastic toys. Factories just make molds, pour in the plastic, and presto—out comes a toy!

Recycled-fabric rag doll, Jamaica

Wooden wheelboard, Colombia These kids have found a way to have fun by hammering together a few old pieces of wood and attaching some wheels.

Clay-and-toothpick cow, Niger The Bororo people are nomadic cattle herders who live in the African country of Niger. This Bororo boy has used clay from the riverbank to create a miniature member of the herd!

Toy aircraft made from soft-drink cans, Vietnam

Stilts, Thailand Bamboo is plentiful in the wet lowlands of Thailand. So it's natural that Thai people would make toys from bamboo. Stilts are among the most popular bamboo toys. Thai children love to balance and play games while walking on their bamboo stilts.

Toys and Beliefs

Want to celebrate something? Maybe it's time to grab a special toy!

In Mexico, donkey toys made from corn husks help kids celebrate the festival of Corpus Christi. The toy represents the pack mules that traditionally arrived in Mexico City from the coast during the time of the festival.

To help celebrate their New Year and bring good luck, the Japanese make *daruma* dolls. Some special wishing *darumas* are made without eyes! Japanese children paint in one eye on the daruma after making a wish. They paint in the second eye only if the wish comes true.

In many places in the world, toys are a way for children to feel like part of the party when there's a big celebration. What kind of toys do you use to celebrate your favorite holidays?

Peruvian grave-offering dolls
These ancient cloth dolls were made to be placed on the graves of loved ones who had died. The dolls were intended to keep the loved ones from being lonely in the afterworld.

***Dreidel,* Israel** During the Jewish holiday of Hanukkah, it is a tradition for children to play a game of chance with a four-sided top called a *dreidel*. They spin the *dreidel*, then watch to see which one of the four Hebrew letters lands on top.

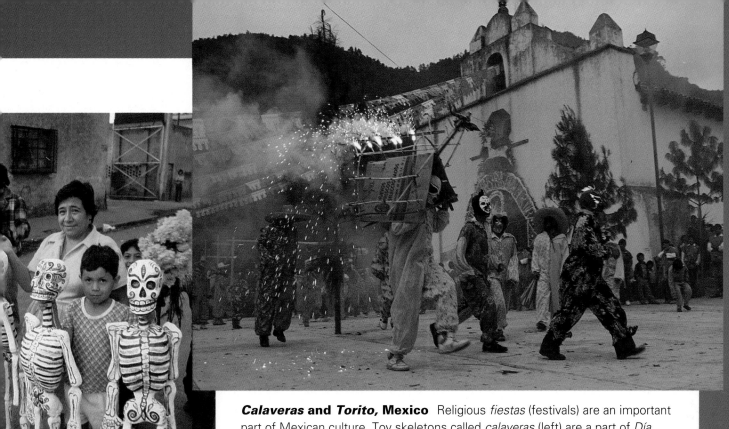

Calaveras and Torito, Mexico Religious *fiestas* (festivals) are an important part of Mexican culture. Toy skeletons called *calaveras* (left) are a part of *Día de los Muertos* (Day of the Dead), a happy celebration honoring the souls of those who have died. The *Torito* (above) is one of the most popular folk toys of Mexico. It is shaped like a bull and filled with fireworks. During *fiestas,* the adults who make the *torito* light the fireworks, place the bull on their head, and then charge into the crowd. The noise and flames delight the crowd.

Daruma dolls, Japan These dolls are named for Bodhidharma (known in Japan as Daruma), the sixth-century Indian monk who founded Zen Buddhism. Legend has it that Daruma sat still and meditated for nine years! The sitting spell supposedly paralyzed him, so he couldn't use his arms or walk. He rolled to other countries like China and Japan to spread his message. *Daruma* dolls have no arms and legs, and always return to an upright position when pushed.

Have a Ball!

Balls are a funny kind of toy. They're so simple—just something round—that it seems like they'd get boring fast. But they don't! Balls are so simple that it seems anybody can figure out fun things to do with them. Balls are among the oldest known toys—and they are found in almost every culture.

Babies and small children like to roll balls to people. Young children like to play catch with their parents. And older kids invent games to play.

Some games are played all around the world—take soccer, baseball, and basketball, for instance. Other games just stay in one country. In Argentina, kids sew leather straps to a ball and toss it around while riding on horseback.

Having a ball is probably the easiest way in the world to have fun.

Crow kicking ball, North America
The Crow people, who traditionally lived on the North American Plains, used balls like this in a game similar to soccer.

Soccer player Soccer is a truly international sport. One of the greatest soccer players ever, Pelé, was so poor growing up in Brazil that he learned soccer by kicking grapefruits instead of soccer balls.

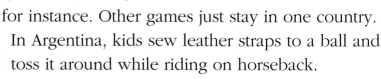

Schoolchildren playing ball, Zimbabwe

Inuit ball, Canada Like the Crow people, the Inuit people also traditionally played a ball game similar to soccer.

Girl juggling balls, Tonga

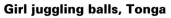

Chinlone **rattan ball, Myanmar**

Chinlone, a popular sport in Myanmar, is played with a hollow ball made of rattan cane. Cane is a plentiful plant in Myanmar's hot, wet climate. Six players stand in a circle and try to keep the ball in the air by using any part of their bodies except their hands.

Wheels, Gears, Wings, and Sails

Some toys are just made to move. They roll, they fly, they sail, they even walk. Wind them up and watch them go. You name a way to move, and there's probably a toy that does it.

Little children like pulling toys on wheels. In fact, "pull" toys have been around for centuries.

Many moving toys are miniature versions of the vehicles people use to get around. Since people use different kinds of vehicles in different countries, toy vehicles vary from culture to culture as well. For instance, in the Philippines, where boat travel is popular, kids carve boats from wood.

Wooden pull-truck, Venezuela

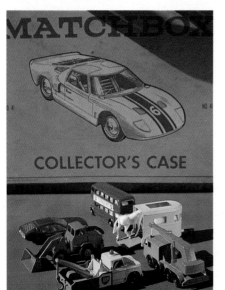

Guess what happened after people started driving cars? Yep, toy cars rolled in.

Toys with wheels and gears are fun because there are lots of different things to do with them. Race them. Watch them fly. Crash them. Even ride them if they're big enough. Just don't let them sit still and collect dust. Keep these toys running!

Matchbox cars, England You've probably played with Matchbox cars. But did you know they got their name because the cars really could fit into a box for matches? British people love motor sports, so it's no surprise that they were among the first to turn cars into miniature toys.

Wooden helicopter, Botswana In the African country of Botswana, helicopters are a familiar sight.

Toy outrigger boats, Papua New Guinea Papua New Guinea is an island country, so people frequently travel by boat. These handmade toy boats are modeled after a kind of boat popular in Papua New Guinea because it doesn't tip over even when the waves are very big.

Tricycle, Russia Riding a bicycle or a tricycle is more than fun. It also helps children develop their muscles! Trikes and bikes can be found all over the world.

Building Mind and Body

No matter where they live, kids like building things. They like to erect tall structures that climb and climb until, whoops, they topple over! In fact, building with blocks is a good way to see how gravity works.

Building and balancing toys are among the many toys that help kids learn. They help children experiment with shapes, test their balance, and use their imagination. With toys like this, kids have so much fun, they don't even know they're playing with a teacher in disguise.

Puzzles and games are also teachers in disguise—they help kids build their "mental muscles"!

Blocks, United States
Simple blocks like these help very young children strengthen their muscles while learning the alphabet at the same time!

Assembling a model toy, Philippines

Legos, Denmark Legos were invented in the 1800s by a poor Danish woodworker who started out by trading his toys for food. Today, Legos are so popular that there's a theme park in Denmark to celebrate them! Children can learn a lot about construction from toys like Legos. Some Lego sets are very complex, with detailed instructions that sometimes take days to complete.

Wooden clown puzzle, Sweden
Puzzles like this challenge children to take things apart and put them back together.

Jigsaw puzzle pieces
Jigsaw puzzles are found all over the world. They stimulate both mind and body, because they teach patience and logic while building physical coordination.

Inuit girl playing "cat's cradle" With flexible fingers and a little bit of imagination, intricate patterns can be made with something as simple as a piece of string. That's why string games are popular in many countries throughout the world.

Strategy game, India With strategy games, the players use logic to beat their opponent.

Dominoes Games are great because they help teach kids patience, logic, and how to interact with other kids. The game of dominoes is very popular in Spain, Italy, and France.

Tinker toys, United States Tinker Toys have changed little since they were first introduced in the United States many years ago. But instead of wood, they're now made of plastic. The shapes haven't changed, though, and kids still like building interesting objects with them.

Rubik's cube, Hungary A Hungarian mathematician invented this toy in the 1970s. The idea is to get each side of the block all the same color. The toy became so popular all over the world that Dr. Rubik became a millionaire!

Let's Pretend

When you were a little kid, did you ever pretend to be a mother or father? How about a lion or a monster? There are lots of different toys for pretend play. Stuffed animals and dolls were probably your first "pretending" toys. Whatever language you learned to talk, you probably uttered some of your first sounds by making your stuffed animals bark, growl or meow.

Puppets are great for pretend conversations and acting out plays with friends. Puppets can be made so easily from scraps of material that they are found in almost every culture. They range from simple finger puppets to wooden marionettes with movable heads and limbs.

Finger puppets, United States
These finger puppets, made of papier-mâché and cloth, could easily be made at home.

Crayfish marionette, Peru Marionettes, found in many cultures, are puppets that are moved from above by attached strings.

Punch and Judy puppets, England Punch and Judy are well-known puppet characters first introduced in England in 1662. They fit over the puppetmaster's hand like a glove. Similar versions of Punch and Judy are popular in other European countries. In a traditional Punch-and-Judy show, the two characters are always quarreling with each other.

Shadow puppets, Indonesia Indonesians love to watch shadow plays called *wayang.* To make the puppets, toymakers cut intricate figures from leather. The puppetmasters stand behind a white sheet, with a light behind them. They put the puppets on long poles, so the figures appear to float behind the curtain. The puppets are so popular that the government sometimes uses puppet shows to spread news across the country.

Puppets and dolls are so common throughout the world because they satisfy the need of all young children to practice talking and use their imaginations. They also help children learn about emotions and caring.

Many pretend toys are just miniature versions of the real-life, everyday objects found in a person's environment. These miniature toys help kids learn about the world around them.

Boys digging miniature wells, Niger When playing pretend, kids tend to make things that they see or use in their own culture. To these Bororo boys—whose families get their water by digging wells— a hand-dug well is a familiar sight.

Make-believe movie camera, Spain

Make-believe musical instruments, Ecuador

Miniature clay tea set, Mexico
Miniature toys, called *pequeñitos* in Mexico, are made of everything from clay to straw to copper by Mexican artisans. Children love playing and pretending with these miniature toys. Many children and adults collect and display them, too.

Stuffed elephant, France Dolls and stuffed animals help kids learn about emotions and caring.

Toys Get Around

Everywhere kids have gone, they've taken their toys with them. Often, toys start off in one country but catch on and become popular in another. In the 1500s, kids in France and England loved riding hobbyhorses—but the first hobbyhorse actually came from China! Nintendo games were invented in Japan, but kids all over the world love them. And kids in lots of countries like playing with Barbie dolls, which originated in the United States.

Latvian kids playing with Barbies
Kids around the world use lots of toys that were invented in the United States. That's partly because they see American toys in movies and television shows that are shown all over the globe.

Hobbyhorse Hobbyhorses have been around for hundreds of years, but they're as popular as ever in many parts of the world.

But sometimes, people on opposite sides of the world just happen to have the same great idea for a toy! The pecking chicken toy is popular in about 20 different countries, but they're all a little different. A toy may work or be made differently because of different peoples' materials, beliefs, or activities—but everyone likes to have fun!

Stuffed bear, Romania Toy bears were popular for years in countries like Germany, Russia, and Romania, where bears roam the woods. Did you know that in the United States, "teddy" bears are named after a president? After a cartoonist drew a picture of Theodore Roosevelt with a tiny bear, parents started naming toy bears after him.

Kids playing marbles, Sumatra The game of marbles is played across the globe—from Sumatra to South America.

Pecking chicken The pecking chicken may be one of the world's most widely traveled toys. Kids hold a paddle, and a weight swinging underneath makes the chicken heads bob up and down. At least 20 countries around the world have their own versions of the toy.

Glossary

aboriginal of or relating to the native people of Australia (p.10)

ancient very old (p.6)

archaeologist a scientist who studies past times and cultures by digging up and examining artifacts such as bones, tools, graves, buildings, pottery, and other human-made objects (p.6)

complex complicated (p.4)

conceal hide (p.9)

coordination the ability to make the parts of one's body work together smoothly (p.5)

culture the beliefs and customs of a group of people that are passed from one generation to another (p.4)

durable able to last (p.13)

encourage to help (p.5)

environment a person's natural surroundings (p.28)

gravity the tendency of objects to fall toward the center of the earth (p.22)

intricate complicated, having much detail (p.24)

joust a formal combat between two knights on horses armed with lances (long, spearlike weapons) (p.6)

logic a way or method of reasoning to solve a problem (p.23)

manufactured made in a factory (p.8)

mass production the process of producing things in large quantities, usually by machinery (p.8)

medieval of or relating to the Middle Ages, the period in European history from about A.D. 500 to about 1500 (p.6)

nomadic of or relating to people who move from place to place instead of settling in one place (p.15)

originated began (p.30)

outrigger a frame holding a float extended beyond the side of a boat to keep it from tipping over(p.21)

prehistoric occurring before the time when humans began recording history through writing (p.6)

rattan the long tough, flexible stem of various palm trees (p.19)

recycle to use a material again (p.14)

stimulate to spur to activity (p.23)

strategy the technique of devising a plan to outwit an opponent (p.24)

superstition the belief that many helpful and harmful supernatural forces exist and that certain actions will please or anger them (p.9)

technology the scientific methods and ideas used in or available to a given culture (p.8)

Index

About the Authors

Cynthia Hedges Greising, a former editor for *The World Book Encyclopedia,* is a freelance writer and editor. David Greising works as the Atlanta bureau chief of *Business Week* magazine. They are both graduates of DePaul University. Cynthia has also done graduate work at the University of Chicago. The parents of two young children the Greisings live in a house filled with toys.